Building an Intergenerational Church

OLDER ADULT ISSUES SERIES

The Office of Older Adult Ministry of the Presbyterian Church (U.S.A.) and Geneva Press are grateful for the generous gifts of many individuals, congregations, and organizations that helped make possible the publication of this series.

Building an Intergenerational Church

Edward A. Loper

Published for the Office of Older Adult Ministry,
A Ministry of the General Assembly Council,
Presbyterian Church (U.S.A.)

Geneva Press
Louisville, Kentucky

© 1999 Office of Older Adult Ministry, Congregational Ministries Division, Presbyterian Church (U.S.A.)

All rights reserved. No part of this book may be reproduced or transmitted in any form or by any means, electronic or mechanical, including photocopying, recording, or by any information storage or retrieval system, without permission in writing from the publisher. For information, address Geneva Press, 100 Witherspoon Street, Louisville, Kentucky 40202-1396.

Portions of this book may be reproduced for not-for-profit use only.

Scripture quotations are from the New Revised Standard Version of the Bible, copyright © 1989 by the Division of Christian Education of the National Council of the Churches of Christ in the U.S.A., and are used by permission.

ISBN 0-664-50088-9

Contents

1. A Changing Landscape — 1
2. Models for Family Tasks — 5
3. The Church as an Intergenerational Community — 9
4. Developing Intergenerational Ministry — 15
5. Baby Boomers in Context — 19
6. Relationships among Generations — 23
7. A Paradigm Shift — 33

Conclusion — 37
Further Reading — 39

1 A Changing Landscape

For the last twenty years or so the Presbyterian Church (U.S.A.) has been a leader among denominations talking about older adult ministry. We have maintained a national presence, challenged presbyteries and synods to include older adult ministry, raised the issue in congregations, and, at the bottom of it, we have challenged individual Presbyterians to think of their aging differently. By and large the effort has been successful.

We have, however, always thought of older adult ministry in certain ways. We have talked about the services needed, or the services we perceived were needed, by older Presbyterians. The conversation has focused particularly on frail and dependent adults, attempting to teach clergy how to minister to them, and putting emphasis on developing nursing home programs. Older adult ministry practitioners have spent a fair amount of energy raising the consciousness of the larger church regarding the needs of older adults. We are aware of ever-increasing numbers. The typical conversation around the table at older adult ministry committee meetings has had a lot to do with "what to do for old folks." We've talked about everything from Elderhostels to nursing home worship with Alzheimer's patients.

Now, the landscape is changing for older adult ministry. Several things have happened:

1. The sheer numbers of projected older adults has forced us to look beyond the what-can-we-do-for-the-old-folks mentality. We are starting to realize that we cannot isolate one group from the whole for intervention. We need to look at older adult ministry as part of a much larger system. People don't live in isolated subsets. Humans live in systems, connected to one another.
2. The economy of America in the last part of the twentieth century has pretty much destroyed the idea of extended family. For several generations, youth have been leaving their communities of origin to follow jobs, and their parents have been moving away from their communities of origin to retire. It is not uncommon for retired parents to be living in Arizona or Florida, with the siblings scattered all across the country, with no one living in the old hometown. Along with the economic and racial distinctions we have always made, we have a whole new system of age distinction. More and more, we live in isolated units that interact less and less with the surrounding community.
3. Baby boomers have been studied since the first one was born. All that study has shown us is that baby boomers are different, have different attitudes, are motivated differently, and will experience their aging differently. There are some real differences

between the generations born before World War II and those born later. One major difference, with ramifications for the church community, is that older generations are motivated by sacrifice and the giving of self as a virtue, while postwar generations are consumers. The motivations for being part of a church community are very different, as are the ideas of what we do once we enter one.
4. We are in the midst of a generational shift in power that calls for intergenerational understanding and solutions.

The focus of older adult ministry has and will change as baby boomers approach older adulthood. While we will still need to focus attention on the old and the frail and the dependent, we will need to expand older adult ministry to include the attitudes of baby boomers as they age, to break down the barriers that have separated generations, and to understand baby boomers and their relationship to the generations that have come before.

An Intergenerational Ministry
My thesis is simple. When we speak of older adult ministry, we really mean intergenerational ministry. When we speak of baby boomers, we speak of the relationship and the connection they have with the generations coming before and after them.

There was a time, not all that long ago, when we did not need to intentionally talk about the relationships between generations. The relationships were plain for all to see. Most Americans lived in the context of an extended family.

Members of several generations lived in a close proximity to one another, knew each other, and supported each other.

This is no longer the case. As noted above, modern economics have changed the notion of extended family. The nuclear family, parents and children, once lived in multi-generational groups. They now exist in free-standing isolation, changing dramatically the relationship among generations and the way we raise children. Specifically, we live in a way that no longer allows for older people and young people to interact with one another. Our culture is poorer for it.

2   Models for Family Tasks

Family has always had an important job to do. There are several models to describe the job. The one I prefer suggests three tasks: (1) to keep children safe; (2) to tell the family story about who we are, where we have come from, and why we are the way we are; (3) to teach children what they need to know to make it in the world, what it means to be a man and a woman, and what it means to live in relationship and community. The job of the family is to transmit the family and cultural values from one generation to another while keeping the children safe.

The nuclear family cannot do this job all by itself. It needs the extended family to help. Each member of the family is involved in separate aspects of the work of raising children. The nuclear family provides for the very immediate tasks of raising a family: putting food on the table, keeping a roof over the head and clothes on the back, and providing for an education. The work of extended family is to provide for the transmission of values and to be a safety net for the family unit.

One place to look is in the inner-city community. Families have been hit hard by changes in the nuclear family. For a variety of reasons, men are standing outside the family unit leaving a huge number of households to be headed by women. A high degree of drug use has impaired the child-raising ability of both men and women. We see a huge network of grandmothers and aunts raising their grandchildren, nieces, and nephews.

I remember stories of my own family taking in both kids and adults who had fallen on hard times. My grandmother always talked about a cousin named Jim. For reasons I never understood, Jim did not work. He was dependent. He moved from relative to relative for support. Every spring he would show up at my grandparents' back door and stay for a few weeks or a month. They would simply set another place at the table and make up another bed until he would move on to another part of the family.

As the kids in the family watched the interdependence and community support, they learned something about family values and relationships. This was especially true in times of family crisis. During illness and death, the extended family provided the support needed to get the nuclear family through the crisis. In fact, illness and death were actually a crisis of the entire community.

I am the only one of our family to have left the hometown. My sister, cousins, aunts, and uncles still live within a few miles. We grew up as an extended family and remain so. Two winters ago, our family experienced the death of my mother—in her home, the home in which my two parents raised my sister and me. Our family handled this death as one might expect an extended family to do. Mother remained home. We all took turns caring for her. Food and everything else we needed was provided and brought in by the neighbors, aunts, and uncles. Nearly all of us were present when she died.

I contrast her death with many of those I have participated in as a church pastor, nursing home chaplain, and hospice chaplain. I have been part of deaths, more often than not, that happen in hospitals and nursing homes because there is no local family to provide the care at home. When deaths do occur at home, it is often with hospice serving as the extended family.

It is very common now, when I am called for a funeral, for the body to be flown in from Florida, for the kids to fly in from their homes around the country, and for the grandkids to fly in from yet other places. I feel sad when I think of that. I remember how good it felt to be among people who had known my mother and me our whole lives, who understood what it meant to be us, and to truly celebrate her life.

Having a sense of extended family is much harder these days. It strikes me at many funerals that there are lots of first cousins who have never met one another.

3   The Church as an Intergenerational Community

Churches are in a perfect position to build the type of intergenerational community that can do some of what extended family used to do. Put another way, there are great benefits in helping kids, their parents and grandparents, young folks and old folks, find each other and share time together.

A Retirement Community
During my days of offering pastoral care at the Presbyterian Home, I saw the following played out in a scene I will never forget. A youth group director had contacted me, looking for a meaningful experience for the kids in her group. I have long held the opinion that manufactured meaningful nursing home experiences for junior high kids are seldom that, and it has always bothered me that we were tailoring those experiences to benefit the kids and not our residents.

This group had a plan. Could I put together a panel of residents who would be willing to field and answer questions put to them by teenagers? I had my doubts but would try. I ended up bribing three women into participating by agreeing to take them out to lunch at a real restaurant if they would sit on the panel.

At first the questions were bland enough. What was it like to grow up back then? What was school like? When did you vote for the first time? Then things started getting personal, and I sat on the edge of my seat waiting to intervene. Were you married? Jane answered no. Why not? I intervened, but Jane said she wanted to answer the question. For the next twenty minutes she held us riveted as she told us about the young man she was engaged to marry and the tremendous grief she felt when he was killed in World War I. She never found another man to measure up. If that was not enough, she finished her story by saying, "Thank you for asking me that question. I've not talked bout this in fifty years, but I guess I needed to." It was not more than a month later that she died, and I think that evening she spent with a youth group had something to do with the quality and peace of her dying.

The church is one place left in our culture where kids and old folks have an opportunity to experience one another in a meaningful way.

A Confirmation Class
The following idea was reinforced by a confirmation class a few years ago. In the confirmation process, we had never really taken the idea of sponsors seriously, a loss for the kids and the sponsors. Sponsors usually ended up being parents who did room mother stuff, provided transportation, brought snacks, and cleaned up.

For this class there were new ground rules. Parents could not be sponsors. Kids had to go out into the congregation to find a sponsor. Help was offered to the introverted. Much to my surprise, nearly all of them came back with an older member.

The sponsors were asked to take the course with the kids and to do all the work. Each assignment asked for a careful reading of scripture, and asked for responses to questions that were designed to reinforce knowledge and interact with issues. Each class had three distinct time frames. Each kid and sponsor talked about the assignment as a pair, then we discussed it as a group, and then we had some didactic teaching time. It was awesome to listen to older adults and teens talk to each other about sex and abortion, justice and politics, death and faith, and what the church and worship is really all about. The talking was awesome enough, but even more awesome was the fact that they started listening to each other and learning.

An Advent Parents' Night

One more vignette. One year we tried to set up an intergenerational experience during Advent. We planned a parents' night out in the context of a covered dish dinner. We asked the older members of our congregation to bring a dish to pass. We bought some pizza and soda and promised a fun and messy activity.

The activity was a gamble. We set out pie pans of tempera paint and a large piece of banner cloth. The idea was to make a full handprint using a favorite color, then sign and date the print. I knew the kids would love it, but I was not so sure about the adults. Not to worry. Almost immediately, five-year-olds and eighty-year-olds were laughing together as they made prints and washed up. It was wonderful. Now we have a banner with some handprints smaller than the hands are now, and a tangible memory of some people who are no longer with us.

The idea is to get older people and younger people spending meaningful time with each other. Ultimately, the point is about transmitting values. Part of our thesis is that the culture has become impaired with regard to the transmission of values from one generation to the next and an intergenerational church ministry can help cure the impairment. To that end, the context of intergenerational ministry is crucial.

For many congregations, the issue of children is an important one. Some congregations that do not have children in their midst see children as a key to their survival. These congregations are the ones that are always looking for a young minister with a family, who will presumably attract more families with children. Members of these congregations talk about youth being the future of the church. The underlying assumption seems to be that if a church does not have children in its midst, it is a dying church.

The argument is a common one and has both flaws and strengths. Its flaws are with regard to its assumptions about older adults. The underlying understanding is that a church without children is somehow a failed, dying community. The truth is, a congregation lives from one generation to the next by evangelism and recruitment and not by simply raising our own children in the faith. Sustaining the community requires more. Moreover, the truth is that faith communities of older adults can be very vibrant and vital communities.

The strength of the argument for our purpose is that in order to have an intergenerational community, the community has to have multi-generations. For churches of one generation, this may take some intentional soul searching and consideration of change.

The temptation is to do a quick job of constructing programming. Programming is important, but it will not do the whole job. The context of the programming is quite important, maybe even crucial. Programming at dissonance with its context will be confusing at best in the attempt to build intergenerational community. A congregation intent on building such a community will need to look at its big picture.

Remember that the point of building an intergenerational community is to try to compensate for the impaired ways in which values have been culturally transmitted. Also remember that a big part of absorbing values for kids is in watching and listening.

So, it follows that if we are to be intentional about using intergenerational ministry to transmit values, we need to be just as intentional about modeling the values we seek to teach. For example, if we seek to teach kids that smoking is not good stewardship of the body while a group of smokers hangs out in the kitchen or by the back door at every coffee hour, what we say is contradicted by what we do.

That is a big problem. With regard to everything we teach or say, we need to constantly evaluate whether we always tell the truth even when it is difficult, whether we are fair and honest in our business dealings, whether we treat our employees fairly, and whether we disagree with one another in a respectful way. None of these things are missed by kids.

About a generation before I came to my present position, the church experienced a bitter fight. Anecdotal history places it at level three on the conflict scale. There is a whole generation of kids who grew up at that time who say they want nothing to do with the church because of what they saw and heard. That's powerful.

To be intentional about intergenerational ministry, we need to do some hard thinking about how family- and kid-friendly we really are. To be clear, this is not about the trend to do market studies on what baby boomers want and to totally redesign ourselves to meet whatever expectation we find in our study. What is called for is an examination of what it means to be faithful within our theological, historical, and liturgical tradition, whatever it may be. It means seeing what we can do in our theological context to be engaging and exciting.

4 Developing Intergenerational Ministry

Here are some ideas of what we need to look at to be family friendly as we develop intergenerational ministry:

- quality nurseries, well staffed, with demonstrated attempts at safety. This means having equipment that is not castoff, and screening the volunteers for histories of crimes against children, no matter how long we have known them or how nice we think they might be.
- opportunities for community and connection
- education that is engaging and transmits values, taught by people who are qualified
- music that is engaging
- preaching and worship that have some life and relevance and provide some sense of pastoral care

How do your statements about valuing children live themselves out in your midst?

- Do children's sermons really seek to communicate something worth knowing, or are the kids props to communicate to adults, or worse, to amuse?
- Are baptized children genuinely invited to participate in the Lord's Supper? And are genuine efforts made to help parents communicate age-appropriate understandings of the sacrament?
- Do we really seek to include children in the life of the congregation, or are we merely talking about it and simply deluding ourselves?

—Do we make real effort to include youth in the decision-making process of the congregation, and do we take care to send them to events such as the Youth Triennium?

To be intentional about building intergenerational community, we need to be asking similar questions about the ministry with older adults in our midst. Even though we have invested the last twenty years or so in trying to break the myths of aging, some myths and stereotypes remain. It will be important to examine our churches to ensure that they are older-adult friendly, especially the churches that are certain they are.

It is critical that we continue the push to look at age in a positive light. A large part of the culture around us continues to see age and aging in a negative light. We still see outrageous stereotypes of older adults in the media. Cosmetics to cover the signs of age are big business still. We still see early retirement incentives offered to people who are just hitting their stride with a whole career of experience still to offer. They are encouraged to retire because they are too expensive and entry-level people can be hired for much less.

A major sign of the health of the anti-aging camp is the tremendous amount of material mourning fortieth birthdays. Take a look at the birthday shelf space dedicated to black balloons and "over the hill" banners.

The church needs to be encouraged to look at aging, all of life actually, in the light of the scriptures and our theology. Age is simply another stage of life to be lived and celebrated. There are some wonderful models of age in the scriptures. Look at how many times God goes to the old folks to get something done. Read the stories about Abraham and Sarah, Moses, Noah, and Jacob with an eye toward what these sagas say about age and wisdom.

Even more, however, we need to take a close look at how well we live out what the scriptures teach us about age. In terms of how well we serve the older adults among us and the quality of role modeling we offer younger folk, there are two areas to pay attention to.

One area is our attitude about retirement. For several generations, coming out of the historical family blip of the 1950s, we have lived out an idea of retirement that pretty much removes older adults from the mainstream. Good jobs, real estate equity, investment opportunities, and pensions have allowed folks to leave the workforce and enter a whole new life. Droves of folks have left homes in the urban north for Florida and Arizona, and lately the mid-South, for a life of leisure. This does two things. It changes the notion of extended family and the ability of older adults and kids to experience interacting with one another. The notion of retirement tends to set up old-age ghettos with an insular way of looking at the world. It also robs the larger community of the wisdom and experience of older adults.

Economics will probably dictate another style of retirement for baby boomers. Many of us in that generational slot wonder and worry if we will be able to retire at all, let alone in the style of our parents and grandparents.

If we look at the idea of retirement through the eyes of

faith and in terms of spiritual development, however, we see something different. Retirement can be seen as the time when we are really free to make a contribution. No longer part of the workforce, older adults can contribute their wisdom, maturity, and experience unfettered. For some that might mean advocating for justice issues. For others it might mean volunteering in programs that benefit the poor and oppressed or in schools. Some find ways to share their professional experience. I have long been impressed by SCORE, the Service Corps of Retired Executives, who share their experience with small-business people at no charge.

A second area we need to address with the community, if we are to sustain ourselves as an intergenerational community, is that of death, loss, change, and suffering. We will need to be very clear about what the faith has to say with regard to these topics. Simply put, we need to be talking about things that matter.

5   Baby Boomers in Context

It is impossible to think of intergenerational ministry without having some understanding of the baby boom generation. This generation will be the focus of older adult ministry in the years to come, and it is essential to understand its relationship to the generations before and after it. Intergenerational ministry will make no sense if the baby boom generation is not understood.

At the beginning of this book, we made reference to the ways in which the church and older adult ministry is changing. With the baby boom generation beginning to pass through middle age, on the verge of older adulthood, the fact that things are changing should not be a surprise.

The baby boomers, defined as the generation born between 1946 and 1964, have occupied center stage since the first one was born. From music to politics, from parenting to economics, nothing they have touched has stayed the same. This is especially true of the church. For quite a few years the faith community has been asking questions about how to attract the baby boomers to our churches and how to keep them involved. We have wondered what they want and how to deliver it. Now the conversation is ready to mature and take a new turn. The baby boomers are poised to move into older adulthood, and we are wondering about what older adult ministry might look like with them.

If all we know about baby boomers remains true, we can expect a changed church by the time they are ready to pass custody of the community on to the next generation. What will that church be like? How does a church run by baby boomers appear? How easy will it be to get there?

It is impossible, of course, to see into the future. We cannot know for certain the answers to these questions, but there are some tools to help us make an educated guess. This book will rely heavily on the historical theory of William Strauss and Neil Howe as we seek to think about the intergenerational context of baby boomers. The boundaries of this book allow for only the most superficial presentation of their theory. Their two books, *Generations* and *The Fourth Turning: An American Prophecy*, should be read independently and in depth. (This book also relies heavily on the principles of family systems theory as applied to organizations and communities. The reader will benefit from gaining some understanding of this model of church relationships.)

It is an aphorism to say that baby boomers are different from any other generation we have known. This has always been the case. It is certain that the trend will continue into older adulthood.

Unique Characteristics of Baby Boomers
Based on educated guesses, the following is a list of ways

that baby boomers might be different from their parents and grandparents in old age:

— Pampered as children, the focus of pediatricians and orthodontists, baby boomers are likely to enjoy good health, although their fast food diet, high in fat, may catch up with them.
— Baby boomers are likely not to want to think of themselves as declining and growing old. We might expect a high need to contribute, learn, and serve.
— There are sharp differences in expectation of the church with the generations that came before them, and there are also sharp differences from the generations that follow. For example, worship for baby boomers' parents has been a spectator activity, while for baby boomers worship is more experiential and participatory.
— The parents of baby boomers, who came of age during the Great Depression and then fought World War II, understand that sacrifice, giving, and saving are virtues. Baby boomers have been raised to be consumers and receivers.
— Baby boomer parents learned politics from listening to the strong and reassuring voice of Franklin D. Roosevelt through the Great Depression and World War II. Baby boomers cut their political teeth in a war that was considered to be unjust and then watched the fall of Richard Nixon.
— Members of the baby boom generation will have a different view of retirement, as they have had a different view of work. Their parents, quite often, signed on with a job and had it for life. There was an expectation that one would have a job for life, with some measure of loyalty between employer and employee. That is no longer the case. A typical baby boomer will have several careers throughout a lifetime.
— Baby boomers will have a different understanding of their

lifespan and of the concept of time itself. Their parents worked with a linear concept of time; one is born, learns and comes of age, works, retires, and dies. Baby boomers understand time in a more cyclical way; one continues to learn new skills, experiences new jobs, retires from work, and learns again.

This list of differences is not exhaustive. It is indicative of the issues that need to be understood if an adequate notion of intergenerational ministry is to be developed.

6   Relationships among Generations

Intergenerational ministry assumes a systemic relationship among generations that must be understood. One way of understanding this relationship is to reflect on the work of Strauss and Howe (*Generations: The History of America's Future, 1584 to 2069*, Morrow, 1991). These historians have developed an understanding of history that helps us understand clearly the relationship among generations. This work is indispensable in developing intergenerational ministry, and in understanding some of the dynamics of the church in the last few years of the twentieth century.

I will try to lay out my understanding of their theory and then apply it to intergenerational ministry.

Four Types of Generations
— There are four distinct types of generations that rotate in sequence through history. In American history, there have been eighteen generations.
— The generation types are idealist, reactive, civic, and adaptive.
— Each generation is somewhat unique with its own perspective and understanding of itself and the events around it.
— If one wants to know something about a generation, it is helpful to take a look at previous generations of the same type.

— The generations are influenced by another cycle of history. There are alternating periods of secular crises and spiritual awakenings that come at prescribed intervals. Generations are defined partly by how they are affected by the secular crises and spiritual awakenings.
— Several generations experience the same point in time, but where they are in their development will affect how they experience and internalize the event. For example, during the Vietnam conflict, a defining point in time for baby boomers, one generation was experiencing elderhood, another midlife, a third rising adulthood, and the baby boomers were in their youth. Each experienced the conflict differently. Talk about Vietnam with a person from the World War II veteran generation and one from the baby boom generation and you may get two very different perspectives.

The four generation types in this theory, idealist, reactive, civic, and adaptive, always appear in this order, cycles repeating one after another. The only exception in American history is in the cycle following the Civil War. The civic generation was nearly obliterated.

The *idealist generation* is born immediately following a secular crisis. In their youth, the members of this generation tend to be quite indulged and pampered, and come of age in the midst of a secular crisis. As rising adults, idealists tend to be narcissistic and self-absorbed. In midlife, the generation tends to become moralistic and puritan. In elderhood, they become visionary leaders through the next secular crisis. Baby boomers are of the idealist generation type.

The last idealist generation we saw was what Strauss

and Howe labeled the missionary generation. This was the generation that provided the leadership during World War II; the generation of Franklin D. Roosevelt and Winston Churchill. They followed the pattern of the idealist generation: they were raised in indulgence during the gilded age that followed the Civil War; as they came of age, they attacked the values of their parents and grandparents in the relentless pursuit of reform; in rising adulthood, the generation became narcissistic and self-absorbed, inventing vacations, automobiles, country clubs, and suburbs; in midlife they became moralistic and concerned about the values of their children and grandchildren, seeking to protect them with such social devices as Prohibition. In elderhood, the missionary generation provided the wise and revered leaders that steered the nation through the Great Depression and World War II.

The next generation in the cycle is the *reactive generation*. They tend to grow up unprotected and highly criticized, while their idealist parents are participating in the spiritual awakening. They mature into alienated and somewhat hostile rising adults, become pragmatic midlife leaders, and maintain respect in elderhood but seldom actually take power.

The last reactive generation is what Strauss and Howe call the lost generation. The lost shows the development of the reactive generation. As youths, the lost were raised permissively and in near neglect. These were the kids who came into the labor market at the turn of the century, fueling the industrial revolution. As they came of age, they were the fodder for the human devastation of World War I. In rising adulthood, the lost generation partied through the Roaring Twenties, much to the disdain of their parents. In midlife, the lost generation was battered by the Great Depression and provided the field level leadership for World War II. As elders, they provided careful leadership, exemplified by the presidency of Dwight Eisenhower.

The reactive generation currently in view is known by a variety of names including Generation X. As a generation, they have felt unwelcome and criticized by their parents. They have known an America quite different from the one experienced by their parents. They lived through the educational experiments of their parents. They are post-Vietnam and post-Watergate. Their economic future is different. Their thinking is different. They were raised differently. Everything is different. As a generation, they feel that they have continually had to live with the leftovers and messes left behind by the baby boom generation.

The next generation in the cycle is the *civic generation*. This is the powerhouse generation in the cycle; the generation that gets it all done. Since their reactive parents grew up relatively unprotected, the civics are very protected. They come of age overcoming a secular crisis, build things as powerful midlifers, and pass through elderhood as busy people, keeping power until it is pried out of their hands. Their leadership is typically attacked in the next spiritual awakening.

In the last few years of the twentieth century, power is

finally shifting from the last civic generation to the baby boomers, making for an interesting time. The transfer of the presidency from George Bush to Bill Clinton, not to mention the election campaign between Bob Dole and Bill Clinton, is an example of how turbulent the transition in power can be. It is movement from one distinct understanding of the world to another.

The current example of the civic generation is the remnant of the World War II GIs. They were protected youth in the booming days of the Roaring Twenties and came of age learning the values of adversity during the Great Depression. When their generation was called upon to give great sacrifices to fight World War II, they went and sacrificed much. They returned and built the infrastructure for a country and fought the Cold War. They put a man on the moon and built an interstate highway system from coast to coast. They fought poverty and put into place a system of entitlement which now benefits them. Their optimism and "can-do spirit" was epitomized by the presidency of John F. Kennedy, who stated most clearly in his inaugural address:

> Let the word go forth from this time and place, to friend and foe alike, that the torch has been passed to a new generation of Americans—born in this century, tempered by war, disciplined by a hard and bitter peace, proud of our ancient heritage and unwilling to witness or permit the slow undoing of those human rights to which this nation has always been committed and to which we are committed today at home and around the world . . . we shall pay any price, bear any burden, meet any hardship, support any friend, oppose any foe to assure the survival and the success of liberty.

It was the values of the civic generation that the baby boomers called into question during the last spiritual awakening, a questioning that is still playing itself out in national life.

The last generation in Strauss and Howe's cycle, the *adaptive generation*, is the hardest to define. Described, adaptive generations grow up as overprotected youth during a secular crisis. They mature into risk adverse and conforming adults, provide moral leadership during a spiritual awakening, and provide influence, with little respect, as elders.

Strauss and Howe refer to the adaptive generation on the scene as the silent generation. This has been a helper generation that has provided much moral leadership but little political power. There have been plenty of senators and congresspeople and supreme court justices, but no presidents. We went from the civic leadership of George Bush, to the baby boomer leadership of Bill Clinton, with no silent leadership in between.

This generation accomplished the civil rights movement and was a passionate advocate for justice, even if it had no way of achieving the justice. Strauss and Howe point out that the theme song of the silent generation could very well be "If I Had a Hammer." The silent generation was/is a transitional generation. Its members were too young to fight in World War II and too old for Vietnam.

Mostly, the silent generation worked and raised their kids; not a bad way to live. They watched somewhat helplessly from the middle of the generation gap as the civics and the baby boomers fought things out. Now, they are retiring, driving RVs with bumper stickers saying they are spending their children's inheritance, and they are.

To recap the four generations of Strauss and Howe's cycle, they include: an idealist generation that tends to live a prophetic lifestyle of vision and values; followed by reactives who are concerned with survival and adventure; followed by civics living a heroic lifestyle of secular achievement and reward; followed by adaptives, who live a quiet lifestyle of influence and expertise.

Application

If we are to understand older adult ministry as an intergenerational ministry, it is imperative that we understand the relationships among the generations. No one generation lives in isolation from the others. No one generation can be understood all by itself.

The decade of the 1990s has been a decade of change in the culture in general and the church in particular. Sometimes the change has been subtle and at other times it has been spectacular. Many arguments and reasons have been given, but the underlying reason seems to be a generational shift in power. Slowly but surely, the civic generation has been letting go of its power, and the baby boom generation has begun to take its power and make the world notice what that power means.

These have been especially tumultuous years for some mainline Protestant denominations. The front and center issue has been the ordination of gays and lesbians to the ordained ministry of the church. But the tumult is broader than that. There is a real questioning of the national ministry of the church, a ministry that has largely been built on issues of peace and justice. There are bitter divisions within congregations between ministers and congregants. The traditional connectional nature of the church is strained, while many parts of the church act more and more congregational. There is less interest in traditional missionary ministries and more interest in doing mission closer to home. Conservatives call for a return to biblical values; liberals say they never left biblical values; evangelicals call to be included at the table. This has been a time of great conflict.

There are many reasons for any conflict, as there are many reasons for the present tumult. The reasons are, by and large, generational. The solutions are also generational. The conflict is generational because it is generated by a very natural shift in power. The civic generation has run the church, as it has run the nation, for a long time. Its day is nearly past, and its power is surely slipping into the hands of the next generation, the baby boomers. As the transition proceeds, conflict is inevitable.

The interest of the civic generation is in structure, and this has been true in the church. The civic leadership has been very concerned with the health of connectional systems, the buildings, the systems, and the polity of the church. Civics have been very concerned about business being done decently and in order. They thrive on committee meetings and General Assemblies and General Conferences. They have been most generous in supporting the corporate life of the church through gifts and hard work.

This attention to the corporate life of the church has been wonderfully enriched by the influence of the silent generation. This generation has never been flashy or powerful, but they have had their influence in the areas of peace and justice.

Through silent influence many networks of specialized ministries of caring and compassion have been built. There is much talk of inclusion and justice among the silents. They, by and large, are very welcoming to ministries dealing with homelessness and hunger, gays and lesbians, women's rights, protection of the environment, racial justice, and much more. While they have not always been totally receptive to maintaining the infrastructure, they have insisted on ministries of peace and justice.

The baby boomer generation comes from a much different place. They have a built-in aversion to institutional structures and systems. While not necessarily opposed to peace and justice issues, they see them in a different light, and their ministry concerns are closer to home.

Two things need to be highlighted in order to understand how baby boomers will understand and run the church. One is that the natural development of an idealist generation leads to moralistic and almost puritanical thinking in midlife and older adulthood, and the baby boomers are quite concerned about the moral health of their grandchildren. On one hand, baby boomers are disappointed with their children and the ways they are raising their grandchildren. On the other hand, baby boomers have had an opportunity to think about their own youth and are anxious for their grandchildren to avoid the excesses they experienced. Both of these ideas will guide the baby boomers' understanding of church life.

It is no surprise that sexual ethics have become a major part of the theological and ecclesiastical discussion in the 1990s. This is an issue that fits very well into the baby boomers' emerging moralism and puritanical outlook. They expect their leaders to be good moral examples to their grandchildren, and they will be uncompromising on the issue. Factor in the baby boom generation's suspicion of institutional authority, lack of denominational loyalty, and an almost necessary repudiation of the civics' and silents' values, and there is great potential for spectacular controversy.

The power shift is a major change in the way one looks at the world, understands ministry, and thinks about church life.

7   A Paradigm Shift

Loren Mead is correct when he talks about a paradigm shift. He talks about a church in the twenty-first century that has completely changed the way it does business: power and ministry lie more in the hands of the laity than the clergy; mission is local and not far from the front door of the church; denominational distinctions are a thing of the past; worship has been transformed. What Mead describes is a church led by baby boomers: remade, reformed, and renewed. There is little of the church as we have known it that will make it into the next century.

The conflict will come as the values and stability of the civic generation, along with the quiet respectability and conformity of the silent generation, meets the vision and no-fear assertiveness of the baby boomers. The result is similar to a cold front plowing into the hot muggy air of deep summer: turbulence, thunderstorms, and tornadoes. The transition of power from civics to idealists can be very stormy and violent.

This is true, too, in denominations and in congregations. The energy of paradigm shift at the denominational level can be seen in the willingness of factions to stake out positions with a win-at-all-costs attitude, destroy people with whom we disagree, withhold per capita and mission funding when we disagree, and home in on narrow self-interest with an intense determinedness, while ignoring any sense of what is good for the whole.

At the congregational level the battle rages over worship styles, leadership styles, and pastoral care styles. For the next few years, we can expect conflict to escalate as more and more congregations populated by civics and silents, who are also the major funding source, are being led by baby boomer pastors. Two different understandings about worship, leadership, and pastoral care can make for some pretty big storms.

One such lightning-rod issue is that of pastoral calling. Most civic and silent generation members who grew up in the church have come to expect regular calling as a pastoral norm. The pastor is expected to put enormous amounts of energy into visiting members of the congregation on a regular basis, with special energy being spent on visiting the sick and shut-in. This is an aspect of congregational life that many civic and silent generation members cherish.

Baby boomers, on the other hand, don't cherish the notion of pastoral calling at all. It is a bother and it is intrusive. They don't understand it. Life is much too busy to entertain someone for an hour with no apparent goal. If one has a problem one wishes to discuss with the minister, an appointment is made to go to her office.

What is one of the first issues that comes up when baby boomer ministers and civic congregations discover they are not on the same page? Pastoral calling is usually one of the first issues on the table. The civics complain that the minister does not call. The minister is wondering what the point of it is and labels calling a waste of time.

A minister once felt the pull of this at performance review time. He served two congregations. One, a church composed primarily of the civic generation, was severely critical of his paucity of pastoral calling. The other, a baby boomer church, praised him highly for not annoying and burdening them with unnecessary pastoral visits.

It seems that much of the conflict we are experiencing is generational. The solution is also one of intergenerational ministry. The solution has something to do with understanding one another in a generational context. This is true in families, in the culture, and in the church. Understanding the generations around us can help ratchet down the volume of conflict.

The first time I presented this material was at a Presbyterian Older Adult Ministry Network conference. It was new material to me. I was not totally convinced of its validity or, more precisely, the value of discussing a secular view of history at a church conference.

As I laid out the ideas of the erosion of extended family and the transmission of values, the historical concept of Strauss and Howe, and then tried to apply them to church life, I saw a hunger come over the group of civics and silents. This made sense to them and they wanted to discuss it. Several extraordinary things happened.

I was struck by the number of people who wanted to express that this particular generational theory helped explain some of the pain and hurt their family had experienced. It helped them understand that the values of their own generation, or that of their children, was not wrong—it was simply different. Not a surprisingly, much of the pain centered around differences of opinion between civics and their baby boomer sons and daughters. A close second was the importance of the church in family life.

A second extraordinary thing came about as the result of a casual remark on my part. In response to a question, I mentioned that I, a baby boomer, had come to respect deeply the sacrifices made by the civic generation during the Great Depression and World War II. It is true, but it has been a long journey. I had come to realize that our generational values were quite different, but I had come to respect the civics and their values a great deal.

Afterward, several men sought me out, and with tears, told me that those were some of the most healing words they had heard.

Currently, there seems to be a great division among the generations. The cultural failure of generations to interact not only hurts children; it hurts all of us. There is a great hunger for generational healing.

Conclusion

Generational healing is the work of intergenerational ministry. Along with the very important work of teaching kids what they need to know to be moral and productive adults, the work of intergenerational ministry is to bring reconciliation to the generations. The work is to help us all understand that we have experienced many of the same events but have experienced them differently. We have different understandings and different values. We understand our faith differently. We are not wrong. We are simply different.

Further Reading

Gambone, James V. *Together for Tomorrow: Building Community through Intergenerational Dialogue.* Elder Eye Press, 1997. Box 142, Crystal Bay, MN 55323.

Sheehy, Gail. *New Passages.* New York: Random House, 1995.

Strauss, William, and Neil Howe. *Generations: The History of America's Future, 1584–2069.* New York: William Morrow & Co., 1991.

———. *The Fourth Turning: An American Prophecy.* What the Cycles of History Tell Us about America's Next Rendezvous with Destiny. New York: Broadway Books, 1997.